Starting young
Principles and practice in
early childhood development

Marion Molteno

Save the Children

How this booklet was written

1. The practical experience...
Save the Children (SCF) works in over 50 countries, and the decisions about which activities to undertake are made by SCF staff in each country. There has for many years been a body of experience of early childhood work in SCF, but not one that was centrally coordinated.

2. Seeing SCF's work in context...
In October 1994, together with Manchester Metropolitan University, one of the divisions of SCF's UK programmes co-hosted an international conference on Early Years. SCF staff from 12 other countries were invited to share their experiences. Here they were able to consider SCF's practice of early childhood work in the light of experience from various fields – local authorities, teacher-training institutes, policy-makers, academics, voluntary and community-based groups, and other international agencies.

3. Debating the issues...
While so many key staff were in Britain, SCF used the opportunity to debate ideas with London-based staff who do not work closely with early childhood development programmes, and who, in some cases, felt unclear about what such programmes are, whether SCF should be involved, and if so in what way. Over 40 people took part in these seminars, and the ideas that were generated – both agreements and disagreements – have been used as the basis for this paper.

4. Drawing together common principles...
Staff from five countries in which early childhood programmes are a major focus worked together to turn the ideas from the conference seminars into coherent shape. The draft was then sent to staff in all other countries where SCF has early childhood programmes, in order for them to provide further examples and to challenge the ideas.

5. Preparing the booklet...
Those who have been most centrally involved are:

India:	Divya Lata, Shireen Vakil Miller
West Bank/Gaza:	Reem Joudah, Julia Gilkes, Frances Moore
Laos:	Vatthana Manaroth, Val Emblen
Philippines:	Mercy Contrares
UK:	Nicky Road, Margaret Westbrook, Tina Hyder
Policy units:	Eva Lloyd, Sophie Laws, Marion Molteno, Sue Stubbs, Katy Swan

The process was coordinated and the final text written by Marion Molteno (education adviser).

Published by
Save the Children
Mary Datchelor House
17 Grove Lane
London SE5 8RD

© *Save the Children 1996*

ISBN 1 899120 30 0

First published 1996

CONTENTS

INTRODUCTION

Save the Children came into existence over 75 years ago in response to the plight of children made vulnerable by war. From the start its aim has been not only to enable children to survive, but also to help create environments in which they may grow and develop normally.

How to do this raises questions that are complex and often controversial. It is not only dramatic events such as wars that make children vulnerable – economic and social pressures can constitute an equally serious threat, and government policies and community attitudes can significantly increase or diminish children's chances in life.

This booklet has a practical aim: to help people who are working in this field to clarify their aims so that they can operate in ways that are more likely to be useful to children, that are locally appropriate, and that will be long-lasting in their effects. It describes some of the lessons that can be drawn from SCF's experience in over 50 countries. A reading list is included for those who want more information, but since people who are non-specialists do not usually have time to read specialist studies, the booklet aims to summarise some essential principles, and to answer the queries most often encountered from colleagues or sceptical observers.

There is, in any case, a problem with much of the academic work available: as in other fields, much of what is seen as established knowledge has come from Western researchers working largely in western Europe and America. While some of their research on child development may be true for all children, some of it is bound to be culture- and situation-specific. In a world dominated by global pressures – economic, technological, political – there is a danger in thinking that one can find universal solutions to social questions.

The approaches discussed in this booklet highlight the importance of building on local strengths. They have been developed in partnership with communities, governments and local organisations, and they draw on practical experience and sensitive observation in many different cultures, often in challenging contexts of poverty, deprivation or conflict. From this diversity it is possible to draw out a few central principles which guide the work, and the values that underlie it.

What emerges clearly is that even in the most difficult circumstances ways have been found for SCF as an international agency to give children a better chance in life; that where this is done in a culturally sensitive and locally appropriate way it can have a greater effect for good than most people imagine; and that the younger the children, the more profound will be the impact.

PART I
THE NEED FOR EARLY CHILDHOOD DEVELOPMENT PROGRAMMES

A 'programme', in international-agency-speak, is a complex set of activities designed to assist a process. The process in this case is the attempt to influence positively the environments in which young children have to grow up, so that their development can proceed as normally as possible.

Why do international agencies get involved in early childhood development programmes? What can they hope to achieve?

1. THE CHILD'S RIGHT TO LOVING CARE

A question of rights

Save the Children has a particularly clear reason for considering children's rights a vital area of work – the organisation's mandate includes an obligation to try to make a reality of the ideals enshrined in the UN Convention on the Rights of the Child, adopted in 1989. It is well known that in most of the societies in which SCF works, children grow up in situations far removed from those described in the convention, and it may be difficult even to refer to the ideals without seeming to be out of touch with reality. But governments all over the world have pledged themselves to try to achieve these rights as far as possible, and this commitment on paper provides an opportunity for organisations such as SCF to help translate policy into practice.

The convention includes three articles that provide the starting-point for early childhood work:

> "the basic human right of children to survive and develop" (article 6);

> "the understanding that society as a whole shares a responsibility to support parents in caring for and raising their children" (article 18);

> "the guiding principles in whatever arrangements are made should be 'the best interests of the child'" (article 3).

It is once we start talking about what those 'best interests' are that things become complicated.

Programme aims and activities

By supporting an early childhood development programme SCF does not make decisions about where children are best cared for. The starting-point is what is actually happening to children in a particular society. Where it is clear that there are unmet needs, SCF tries to support processes within that society which might lead to more positive environments for children. Here are a few examples of what these processes might involve:

- working to support hard-pressed families so that they can be released to care for their children.

- working to achieve more effective collective childcare arrangements.

- cooperating with community groups who run pre-schools to improve the chances that the pre-schools will encourage children's development rather than restrict it.

- working with governments to research changes in patterns of childcare because of shifting economic conditions, so that appropriate policies can be put in place to deal with new challenges.

While the focus in all these programmes is what is happening to children, the actual activities almost always centre on the understanding and attitudes of key groups of adults. This is because it is adults who are responsible for creating or changing the situations in which children grow up. An early childhood development programme will, therefore, involve discussions and experiences aimed at spreading a better understanding of how children develop and enabling adults to develop the skills to influence children's environments in positive ways. In particularly difficult or deprived situations, the aim may be to find ways of supporting communities to minimise the damage that might otherwise be done to children's development, and to provide positive experiences to strengthen their resilience.

So the umbrella term 'early childhood development programmes' covers a vast range of possible activities which can involve parents, childcare workers, trainers, pre-school teachers, health workers, government officials and policy makers. Naturally, each programme is likely to have an impact on only a few of the factors which affect children, and it is important to see any such work as complementing that of many other agencies, governments, voluntary groups and individuals.

Child development – a cross-cultural view

All children have the same basic needs and the same physical and emotional make-up, therefore there are things we can say with confidence that all young children need if they are to develop normally. But experience of work in many countries has taught SCF staff to take a broad view of the detail of children's needs and capacities, and not to judge situations in one country or community by the standards of another. SCF tries to let the situation itself – and the people who live and work in it daily – define the appropriate ways of approaching the task.

Even the words used most frequently when talking about young children's development may mean different things in different contexts. So it may be helpful to begin by clarifying how SCF staff have come to understand them through their work.

'*Childcare*', or 'being sure that children are well cared for' are words often used when people are thinking primarily of physical care – feeding, safety, health. But they also have a wider use, better conveyed perhaps by the phrase 'loving care' – meaning all that a young child depends on in order to develop normally. Love and emotional security from a few key adults are as important as physical care. We all know this from common sense – but it is highlighted by studies of babies in institutions that provide physical care but little individual attention, stimulus or love. Such babies often have severely retarded development, and are more likely to die young.

'*Education*' is another word with a confusingly wide meaning. To many people it means school, and they may find it odd to hear others talk of the 'education' of children too young to go to school. Sometimes they assume that what is meant is some form of school for younger children – pre-school, kindergarten, etc. SCF uses the word in a more fundamental way to mean the whole learning experience of a young child, which begins at birth (or before). In considering 'early childhood education' it is important to be clear which factors encourage or discourage learning. Babies have a natural capacity to learn, but this capacity can be damaged by adverse circumstances. A child will learn to walk without an adult to teach him or her, and will succeed in learning to walk despite constant discouragement ("Be careful – you'll fall"). But other learning capacities may be more easily suppressed by unhelpful interventions from adults, and studies show that children learn much more effectively in some environments than others. The role of adults, therefore, is to understand the child's natural learning processes and to work with them, not against them.

'*Development*' is the whole ongoing process, involving both loving care and learning. Young children are constantly growing and changing – physically, intellectually, in their ability to take account of others as well as themselves. They become increasingly competent and independent, and develop as creative, emotional, spiritual beings. Key factors in this process are the growth of confidence, the capacity to take responsibility, and the maturity to cope with difficult feelings. These are *not* luxuries for children in the individualistic rich countries. They are survival skills, present in different forms in children in all societies, and even more necessary to children who have to survive in pressured or deprived situations.

'*Early childhood*' isn't a precise set of ages. People use to mean any time from birth until the age at which, in that society, children might be expected to go to school.

(if there is a school). But many of the principles apply to children past that age – in fact, some apply throughout life. As a general rule, the younger the child, the more intensely the principles apply. All children are vulnerable, but younger children are more vulnerable than older ones. The fact that young children can do less on their own hides from many adults the equally important fact that they have the greatest potential for development, and are more deeply affected by the situation they are in, positive or negative.

In the examples of SCF's work given in Part III, the age span of participants is wider than people used to a more limited Western view of 'early childhood' might expect. Child development studies undertaken in Europe or North America often suggest a more uniform pattern of child development than is actually the case. It is recognised that a child who has been denied vital experiences early in life may need to have them much later than would be expected. For example, a child who has been neglected in early life may be unusually attention-seeking at an age when other children have become more self-sufficient. What is less widely recognised is that the variety of childrearing patterns in different cultures means that children have different experiences of life in their first years, and their development reflects this. A study in Uganda showed that African children carried on their mothers' backs developed faster in their first year than European children in the same African environment who spent a lot of time in a cot. Children who are sent off on their own to herd animals from an early age become adept at problem-solving, and capable of a level of responsibility that would stagger child development specialists in the West. But they are unlikely to develop linguistically as fast as children who are constantly with adults. Children of nomadic communities whose first experience of school is at the age of eight may find it difficult to deal with being in a building, sitting still, holding a pen, while much younger urban children can do these things easily. Many children never go to school and never see books, and specifically school-type skills, such as recognising the symbolism of pictures, may be ones they don't develop until much later than children who

do go to school. A girl growing up in a Western city does not learn to walk with the degree of coordination required for carrying things on her head, which an African girl child learns young.

Families, communities and childcare

Save the Children has a commitment to try to bring benefits to children *in the communities in which they live*. This is the organisation's policy, but it is also backed up by everything that is known about child development. Whatever type of programmes SCF supports, they need to be ones which recognise, respect and are informed by local styles of childrearing, unless it is clear that these are not 'in the best interests of the child'.

In most societies there is a strong feeling that the natural social unit in which children should grow up is a family. But 'family' means different things in different societies. A family may be a mother as the sole income-earner and adult carer of four young children, or it may be an extended family of three generations, in which many adults have a role in caring for all the young children. Children may be looked after by grandparents or older siblings, or sent far away to be with an aunt or uncle. The range of 'normal' arrangements for bringing up children is vast. There have been studies of the effects of different types of family or community childcare arrangements on children, and while it is clear that the type of arrangement definitely has an effect (just as, for instance, a child's position in a nuclear family – first, last or middle child – has an effect), it is impossible to say which is 'better' for children. Children may survive and thrive, or not, through many kinds of upbringing – provided certain basic conditions are met.

Common sense tells us that not all families are happy ones. In all societies there are children who are abused or exploited by adults who have authority over them. Arrangements are made without consulting children and they often cause harm. In situations where adults are having to meet conflicting economic and family demands, individual children's needs may be sacrificed, and children are commonly neglected or harshly treated by adults too tired and oppressed to have the energy to consider anyone's needs but their own. Some of the rights of the child as expressed in the UN convention do not form part of the culture of childrearing in many societies, and may actively contravene normal behaviour in a society – for instance, the child's right to freedom of expression (article 13).

Just as it is naive to assume that all families are happy ones, it is also unhelpful to have romanticised views of the ways communities operate and how this affects children. Communities all over the world – at many different income levels and with many different kinds of childcare arrangements – can provide children with their most basic necessity: loving care. Without being aware of it, children in such situations learn many of the essential skills for life as adults in their particular community and environment. But such ideal situations are increasingly rare. Communities are under pressure from poverty, rapid urbanisation, a changing economic system, environmental degradation, war, displacement and the impact of Aids. As a consequence, traditional community and support systems cannot function as they once did. The greater the pressure, the less likely it is that children's basic needs will be adequately met. It is in such situations that a programme which encourages the development of collective responsibility for caring for young children is most needed.

When a programme involves collective childcare – in crèches, pre-schools, kindergartens, collective homecare support – it raises specific types of problems, but also offers new possibilities. One of a child's most basic needs is for individual attention, and that may not be easy to provide in a situation where too many children have to be cared for by too few adults. On the other hand, all children need the company of others and thrive on the stimulus that good collective childcare can provide. Although collective childcare itself may in some societies be a break with tradition, it is vital for the children's well-being that the extent of this break be minimised. Ideally, the style of childcare should not detach children from their communities but enable them to develop within them. A good early childhood programme necessarily involves parents and carers, with particular understanding of the pivotal role of women.

2. THE IMPORTANCE OF STARTING YOUNG

Is early childhood provision a luxury?

Save the Children often encounters the view that early childhood provision is something that can be afforded only in industrialised societies. In fact, even in countries such as Britain good childcare provision is only available for a minority, and SCF battles to persuade policy makers of the need to make it more widely available.

In countries where children are disadvantaged through extreme poverty, disaster or war, work that aims to respond to young children's needs is often seen as an 'extra' and even as a 'luxury'. Governments which have traditionally subsidised some form of childcare will cut early childhood provision before other sectors as soon as they are under financial pressure. Although there may be protestations of regret, they seem to feel it is self-evident that where resources are limited they should not go to very young children.

By contrast, all experience points to the conclusion that ignoring the needs of young children is extremely short-sighted and sure to bring later problems. It is precisely for the very poor, or in societies in crisis, that working with young children is most crucial.

An opportunity we can't afford to miss

There is an important link between what we understand about a child's individual growth, and wider development challenges. Children's first years (0-5 years) are their most formative ones:

> "The growth of the brain during the first few years of life is unmatched by any other developments that occur during the lifespan. Within the first three years infants learn the basics of human behaviour."
>
> (*Why Children Matter*, 1994)

As anyone who has observed young children knows, many aspects of character form early, and many of the social values that will stay with children for years to come are transmitted while they are very young. What is less well understood is the extraordinary learning capacity of very young children, and the fact that patterns of *how* children learn begin to form as early as any other behaviour patterns.

This makes early childhood a time of opportunity when even small positive changes can generate long-term benefits. Events experienced at a very young age are likely to have a lifelong effect, whether you remember them or not. This is usually obvious when we think of the 'loving care' aspects (for instance, the effect of the early death of parents), but it is equally true of learning. Some of the positive effects of good early childhood programmes are immediately evident; the more fundamental effects go on maturing within children and communities over a long period of time and are therefore extremely difficult to measure. But experience demonstrates and research confirms that resources spent at the outset may result in significant long-term benefits and the avoidance of many later problems. Where children are seriously disadvantaged, for example in areas of extreme poverty, in conflict situations, through society's attitudes to their disability, or by being in some other way marginalised, there are strong arguments for offering support at the earliest possible stage.

Early learning and what happens in school

An assumption held in many societies is that the education of very young children is less important than what will happen to them when they are older. Therefore, the logic goes, countries and organisations that are short of resources, but want to do something useful for children's development, should concentrate on school-age children.

Though adults may remember only fragments of what happened before they went to school, events in the first years of life have an immensely powerful formative effect. Learning *how to learn* matters much more than

the actual items of information learned, and patterns of learning (self-confidence, openness to new ideas) begin to be established long before school. Helpful patterns are easier to encourage in the kinds of informal settings in which young children are commonly cared for than in schools. Put starkly, if there are resources to fund a positive learning experience for only three years in a child's life, children will benefit more by having that good experience early.

In practical terms, an organisation of SCF's size and history may in many situations be more likely to make a difference to what happens to children at a younger age than through the school system (which may be very resistant to change) – and that difference is one that may have a more profound effect long term. Of course, it will be distressing if children who have had a good early childhood experience have no chance to go on to school, or go to a school which damages rather than helps their development, but a positive early years' experience will have given them something invaluable that no one can ever take away from them.

'Invest early, save later'

In industrialised societies, arguments in favour of investment in early years' education are often made on the grounds of cost savings to society. Early childhood development activities are said to result in a pay-off for disadvantaged children in higher academic performance, lower delinquency rates and better earnings prospects. These findings, from the High/Scope Foundation's Perry Preschool Study, and from other studies, demonstrate that a good pre-school experience not only prevents problems that would eventually cost society much more than a pre-school programme, but also that it increases the effectiveness and efficiency of the social investment already made in schooling.

Any attempt to substantiate similar claims for poorer countries would be a futile exercise, not least because the statistics do not exist. In any case, other lines of argument are seen as more important to SCF. Well-founded early childhood work responds to children's immediate needs and, at the same time, challenges entrenched patterns of discrimination and disadvantage.

Poverty is the constraint within which all SCF work takes place and there are no magic answers to the challenges it presents. *The Anti Poverty Strategy report*, produced by SCF's Scottish division, concludes that early childhood work is one of the best ways to minimise the problems caused by extreme poverty, and this is supported by numerous studies. At the level of family income, the argument is that "providing childcare is one of the most effective ways of relieving poverty … because of its impact on women's earning power" (Cohen and Frazer, 1991). Perhaps even more significant in the long term, good support at an early age is one of the few strategies known to be effective in breaking patterns of disadvantage.

Early childhood work as a social mobiliser

From a development perspective, work around early childhood issues opens up many creative possibilities. Because children represent the future and hope for change, activities aimed at giving them a better chance in life can act as a powerful social mobiliser. People who have lived under political oppression, who are marginalised economically, or who may feel helpless about changing their situation in other respects will often respond more actively to the vision of trying to change things for their children. In so doing, they bring about changes in themselves. A good example of this was a project in an impoverished fishing village in Colombia where an early childhood programme was established in 1977. Not only did it lead to direct benefits for the children (more of them completed primary and secondary school), but adults became involved in a constantly widening set of self-help activities. "The communities, the children, the mothers, the families, together we have created a new way of thinking, a new way of living and of resolving our problems, problems that are of very great urgency" (Chetley, 1990). These benefits have had an impact far beyond the original community, leading to government support for early childhood programmes nationwide.

Children's needs cannot easily be compartmentalised; development programmes with a strong early childhood component tend naturally to a holistic approach, in which the adults involved become increasingly aware of the interrelations between all aspects of development – social, emotional, physical and intellectual. This in turn acts as a productive stimulus to development work generally.

Building on strengths

Development programmes are sometimes designed according to what people lack (water, food, skills). Well-conceived early childhood work builds on what is already there, strengthening existing skills and practices that have evolved over generations. Early childhood programmes have evoked unusual levels of enthusiasm and energy in communities all over the world; income-generation programmes that focus on childcare and related needs are likely to be more sustained than those that do not.

Such activities can also serve to bring together various groups in a community. The people involved may be from different cultures, religions or social groups and under normal circumstances would not work together to achieve shared goals. But the well-being of children is a common concern and cuts across all these barriers, encouraging participation from all sections of a community.

PART II
CHILDREN'S LEARNING AND HOW TO SUPPORT IT

There is no best way to work in early childhood development; what is appropriate and effective depends largely on the specific context and opportunities. However, there are some basic principles that need to be understood if the work is really to bring benefits to children. Despite the diversity of cultures and situations, there is a remarkable degree of shared understanding among SCF's early childhood workers across the world as to what these guiding principles are.

1. UNDERSTANDING HOW CHILDREN LEARN

For children everywhere, the early years are a time of constant growth and change. Early childhood programmes need to incorporate an understanding of how children learn and develop, and should aim to bring about a greater knowledge of these processes among the adults who work with children. The style of early childhood provision which grows out of this understanding is often said to be based on a Western model. It is naturally one of SCF's concerns to be sure that it is not simply pushing a cultural import. However, there are certain things that seem to be universally true about how young children learn.

Learning at different stages

Observations of how young children approach learning show clearly that they are not ready for learning through abstract symbols such as numbers, but have a highly developed ability to learn in concrete ways, through what is often called 'discovery'. Early learning methods build on these natural processes, enhancing the child's ability to learn from his or her environment. Counting with stones is more fun than reciting tables, and more effective.

Process versus product

A central feature of childhood learning (*all* learning, in fact) is that the *process* is more critical than the immediate product. The aim of most early learning activities is more to develop an active approach to learning than to get

children to absorb a body of facts. Children who are pushed too early to learn in formal and abstract ways may impress adults with their 'knowledge' but do not develop the skills and confidence to take advantage of later learning opportunities, or to learn effectively from life. Not all pre-schools give children a head start in learning. For example, a pre-school which crams children into a small room where they must sit passively for hours learning by rote, damages every aspect of the children's development.

Starting from what is known

Although child development follows certain patterns, the development of an individual child is a unique experience. A child's learning begins at birth and continues constantly. This is easy to say, but its implications need to be acted upon by adults whose job it is to help children learn. What a particular child knows or can do will be constantly changing, therefore the learning situation must be flexible. A predetermined inflexible syllabus, in which all children in a group are expected to do the same things at the same pace, is by definition going to be aimed at an inappropriate level for many in any group. While children through the ages and in all societies have survived such unhelpful types of schooling, it makes no sense to spend scarce resources on a method of teaching that is not linked to knowledge of child development and the way children learn.

Learning by doing, and through play

Children – like adults – learn most successfully by actually doing, rather than by being told. Everything children do in their early years involves learning. Playing on a river bank involves experimenting with water and sand, introducing basic concepts of science. Formal learning can make this understanding explicit, but cannot substitute for the concrete experience. Children have a *need* to experiment, and will do so if unfettered by adults trying to push them into less natural approaches. They use repeated experimentation and imitation, trial and error, to make sense of their experiences and build knowledge. By playing with other children, children learn to interact, negotiate and to deal with feelings and conflicts. Play also helps children to develop their imagination and creativity.

When adults understand the value of children's play, they are more likely to provide space and time, and encourage opportunities to explore the environment. The young baby or immobile disabled child will only do this if cared for in an environment with interesting things to explore. As mobility increases, children begin to search for more experiences in the community. Besides understanding their world by doing, they also try to explore, by copying, the roles of adults. Role-play and fantasy are important in helping children to understand and make sense of the impact of adults around them. In societies where violence and oppression are widespread, this aspect of play is vital to help children express their confusion, fear and anger.

When children are collected together in groups, in a pre-school perhaps, adults often organise collective activities. In the best cases these activities stimulate children to learn and develop, but if inappropriately conceived, they can deprive children of opportunities for natural learning. A good pre-school curriculum tries to leave plenty of space for children to explore and develop their own activities, and substitutes for natural experiences (e.g. the river bank) by using specially collected objects that can serve as learning materials (e.g. a tub of water with various objects which float or sink).

Love and security

Children cannot learn effectively when they are hungry, frightened, anxious about being accepted, or made to feel insecure. The fundamental task of early childhood work is to support processes which will be likely to give children loving, responsive, and non-violent environments. The most important element in good childcare is the presence of interested adults – and *enough* of them to ensure that children are known and loved as individuals.

2. EARLY LEARNING AND TRADITIONAL EDUCATION

Trying to build early learning programmes that are firmly based on an understanding of how children learn brings potential collision with traditional ideas about education in most of the countries where SCF works.

Can *young* children learn?

It is common for adults in all communities to think of young children's needs primarily in terms of physical care. The idea of very young children 'learning' is often new to people who are used to thinking of learning mainly as something that happens in schools. Once the idea of pre-school as a 'learning' place takes hold, it may have a negative effect, with parents expecting very young children to be taught things that are inappropriate for their development stage.

Can *all* children learn?

There is no clear dividing line between disabled and non-disabled children in terms of their learning and developmental needs. Yet the idea that every child is capable of learning is not always accepted. SCF disability programmes worldwide encounter cases of children with disabilities being kept at home, or in special institutions, denied the normal stimulus which would help them learn.

Often it is assumed that children with obvious disabilities will not benefit from attending organised activities such as a pre-school unless there are special facilities. For a blind or hearing-impaired child – or any disabled child – just being with other children will in itself have strong benefits, not only for them, but also for other children who learn to relate to disabled children and care for each other. Of course, such children would benefit from some specialist knowledge about how to encourage learning, to develop language skills, or signing. Appropriate aids (spectacles, hearing aids, mobility aids) would also benefit certain children. Until these can be made available, however, it is still much better for the children to receive general stimulation than to be lying on their backs at home.

Is 'play' a Western concept?

Experienced early childhood workers in all cultures stress the importance of learning through activity or play. But the word 'play' can suggest the concept of childhood as a time when children should be carefree and do what they like, and this is often rejected as a Western approach. In many societies, children are expected to share family responsibilities from an early age, and in this respect often develop more quickly than their more economically privileged Western counterparts, who may be kept in a state where they are not trusted with responsibility long after they are ready for it. The concept of children learning through 'play' is not intended to suggest that a Western style of prolonged childhood is appropriate to all societies. Rather, it is used to alert adults to the fact that the apparently idle activities of children have an important developmental purpose.

Aren't the traditional ways better?

Most cultures have two traditional ways of passing on knowledge and skills to children. One is to let children learn by copying, doing, and being instructed by adults and older children. The other is the tradition of passing on rather specific types of knowledge, such as religious instruction (learned from a master by rote learning).

On to this existing base has been added a system of formal schooling, usually modelled on that of the colonial powers. This was introduced at a time when Western approaches to education were very didactic, emphasising teaching rather than learning, with children passively accepting what the teacher taught them from a pre-decided syllabus. Our current understanding of how children learn has brought about a great (though by no means universal) change in attitudes to schooling in the West, but not in most of the countries in which SCF works. When parents and teachers are anxious for children to learn conventional school-type knowledge, and to learn it in the old way, a particular challenge is to try to put across that children get on better if basic concepts are learned through activity and discovering for themselves, rather than through rote learning.

3. QUESTIONS OF CULTURE

Different attitudes to what is good for children's education highlight important wider issues of culture.

Culture as the child's environment

Culture can mean different things in different contexts. It includes social and religious practices, health practices, language, beliefs, values and knowledge. It is the way people behave with each other, men with women, adults with children. It is impossible to consider questions of childcare without rooting them in a particular culture.

As an international NGO, it is particularly important that SCF is aware of the need to work through local communities, while always recognising that no community is homogeneous. The need for sensitivity to issues of culture applies even though all the facilitators of a programme may be locally appointed staff, for where the work is with very disadvantaged communities there is often a wide cultural gap between people in those communities and well-educated, middle-class programme workers.

Language and culture

Language is crucial, both as a carrier of culture and as the means through which individuals express themselves. Though many communities use several languages, usually for rather specific contexts, young children need first to build a confident ability to use the language which is most immediately used around them. An ever-increasing linguistic ability is a vital part of the early learning process, and research makes it absolutely clear that it is damaging to young children's development to put them in situations where that natural ability is blocked, either because they are unable to make sense of what is being said around them, or not themselves being understood.

Early learning programmes need to be structured in such a way that, wherever possible, all children can operate in the language they are most familiar with. The simplest way to do this is to select childcare workers from the same community. In very deprived communities it is sometimes suggested that this is difficult to do, because there are few literate people who can be trained. Looking after children requires many skills, but literacy is not necessarily one of them, and there is no correlation between being a good child-carer and having a formal education. What is essential is an understanding of child development. It is a challenge to trainers to find creative approaches that do not rely unduly on the written word or on technical language.

Finding ways to use the child's mother tongue is more difficult in situations where there is a range of first languages among the children in a group. Often, all these languages cannot be reflected in the choice of child-carers. Multilingual pre-schools in the UK have developed strategies for this situation, and there are many simple devices for making sure that the languages of all cultural groups are recognised and reflected in the programme. When children from a linguistic minority are having to spend much of the day operating in a language they do not yet feel comfortable with, even one song in their own language (which all the children can learn) can release tension and enable other learning to happen more easily. An obvious starting-point is to involve parents from a linguistic minority in their child's education. This has happened in the UK where parents join workers in developing games for use both at home and in pre-school settings.

Parents, carers and cultural values

Young children learn from those closest to them, and they in turn are influenced by the values of the community. A culture's values and attitudes are a vital part of how a child will experience life. In cases where the child is partly cared for away from the family, it is very important that there should be as much contact as possible between the two environments.

But culture is never static. It is constantly changing, partly through natural processes, partly through the impact of external pressures. Within a community there are almost always sub-cultures with their own complex structures, which give rise to conflicts of interest. This makes the question of 'community control' a complex one. Once it is accepted that early childhood programmes give children a better start in life, there is a danger of their being co-opted by those in the community who are better off. Ways have to be found of ensuring that the programme continues to benefit the disadvantaged community it was set up to serve.

Cultures undermined

Disadvantaged communities are particularly vulnerable to cultural change being forced on them, through economic migration, military occupation, or ethnic or religious oppression. This loss of heritage is often a critical feature of a community's demoralisation, and fostering confidence in one's own culture can be a vital aspect of early childhood work.

The decision about which language to use may be a highly political one. The same goes for food, songs and dances. Some groups may resist any recognition of the cultures of people seen as not 'belonging' – migrant workers, refugees, or those with a traditionally nomadic lifestyle. It usually requires a clear decision on the part of childcare workers to make sure children and parents from all communities feel welcomed on an equal basis.

Culture as a negative force

Cultural influences can be damaging, and in direct contradiction to the rights of the child. A common example is the belief in many cultures that it is unimportant to educate girls. Another is that it is part of a teacher's role to beat a child who does not progress well. There can be no escaping the fact that SCF programmes need to find ways to challenge these practices – but sensitively, from within the community, and by means which are as culturally acceptable as possible.

PART III
DESIGNING PROGRAMMES THAT BRING LASTING BENEFITS

1. AFFECTING THE CONTEXT

Early childhood programmes seek to influence the contexts in which young children live so that their natural development can take place unhindered, and their potential be realised. It is particularly important to know how to approach this task in situations of scarce resources, and where communities are under pressure.

Working with adults who care for children

Since it is adults who decide what kind of environment to put the children in, an early childhood programme needs to help *adults* understand children's developing needs and potentials. This cannot be achieved simply through training a particular set of professionals – health workers or pre-school teachers, for instance. All those who care for children or make policies that affect them should ideally have this understanding. And foremost among these are the adults who have the greatest responsibility for the children, i.e. the parents, or whoever takes the role of primary carer for a particular child.

One of the most productive aspects of a good early childhood programme is the empowering effect it has on adults. Many of the learning principles which apply to children – and can be directly observed in them – apply equally to adults, though they are sometimes more difficult to observe because adults' lives are more filled with complex distractions. Once adults have begun to understand these developmental processes in children, they often move rapidly to understanding the potential for change in their own lives.

Complementary approaches

In his book, *Toward a Fair Start for Children*, Robert Myers highlights five main areas of activity for early childhood programmes. These are complementary approaches – whichever is chosen as the focus of activities in any given situation, it is important to seek ways of using that experience to influence what happens in the other environments affecting the child.

Below is Myers' outline of these complementary programme approaches:

1. Attending to children in centres. The immediate goal of this direct approach, focusing on the child, is to enhance child development by attending to the immediate needs of children in centres organised outside the home. These are, in a sense, alternative environments to the home.

2. Supporting and educating caregivers. This approach focuses on family members and is intended to educate and empower parents and other family members in ways that improve their care and interaction with the child and enrich the immediate environment in which child development is occurring rather than provide an alternative to it.

3. Promoting community development. Here, emphasis is on working to change community conditions that may adversely affect child development. This strategy stresses community initiative, organisation, and participation in a range of interrelated activities, to improve the physical environment, the knowledge and practices of community members, and the organisational base allowing common action and improving the base for political and social negotiations.

4. Strengthening institutional resources and capacities. There are many institutions involved in carrying out the three approaches mentioned above. In order to do an adequate job, they need financial, material and human resources with a capacity for planning, organisation, implementation, and evaluation of programmes. Programmes to strengthen institutions may involve institution building, training, provision of materials, or experimentation with innovative techniques and models (improve the 'technology' available to them). They may also involve providing the legal underpinnings for proper functioning of the institutions.

5. Strengthening demand and awareness. This

programme approach concentrates on the production and distribution of knowledge in order to create awareness and demand. It may function at the level of policy makers and planners, or be directed broadly toward changing the cultural ethos that affects child development.

SCF supports a wide range of programmes, with experience of working at each of these five levels. Examples are given in the sections that follow, to highlight the diversity of contexts and approaches.

2. WHICH CHILDREN HAVE MOST NEED OF SUPPORT?

Child development as a continuous process

Different programmes may be aimed at specific age groups, but for all programmes it is important to understand what has gone before and to influence what will follow.

■ The first years, 0–3

In addition to being the period of the greatest potential development, these first years are also particularly vulnerable ones for children – in terms of actual survival as well as in potential damage if the conditions for normal development are not assured.

From three continents, SCF staff report situations of extreme poverty in which very young children are locked in homes to keep them from straying while their parents or carers are out at work. They also describe children who are regarded as 'abnormal' being isolated from others, and deprived of the stimulus and human contact that is essential for growth. Although people everywhere love babies, societies vary greatly in their understanding of the importance of the first years. In addition to providing essential care for particularly vulnerable children, a good childcare programme which involves parents centrally can have a powerful role in preventing disadvantage for many others through helping to raise adult awareness.

India: SCF supports many NGOs that work with poor communities in remote rural areas. In these communities parents are under such economic pressure that it is often impossible to provide adequate care for very young children. The men migrate to the cities for employment. This leaves almost all the farm work to be done by the women alone. They usually have to travel long distances to collect fuel, fodder and water in addition to doing other household chores and the regular agricultural activities. In one area of Andhra Pradesh women report that the biggest problem they face in caring for their young children is the time it takes to fetch drinking water for the household – sometimes they are able to get only a bucketful in about three to four hours. In the hill districts of Uttar Pradesh it was common practice to leave young children unattended and tied to cots at home when parents were not able to find anyone to take care of them while they were away at work. Once *balwadis* (childcare centres) were started in the villages, they became a focal point for increased community awareness of the needs of children.

■ Years 3–6

From three to six years is the most common age group for early childhood programmes, perhaps because these are years when, in most societies, children begin exploring and developing outside the home environment and adapt easily to being in more organised peer group settings. It is a period of special opportunity when children are usually curious, with an open, eager approach to new activities, and very responsive to positive stimulus.

There are debates in many of the countries in which SCF works about what is best for children of this age. Should they be at home, or in an informal playgroup, or in a nursery class as a preparation for school? Money is usually a dominant factor in the minds of policy-makers. Part of SCF's role is to make sure that concern with what can be afforded does not make those in authority ignore what is good for children and the whole community.

SCF also tries to find ways around the shortage of resources and to promote a flexible approach. Children's development can be supported in many different ways by promoting home-based projects, supporting groups of childminders, establishing hospital playschemes or influencing the authorities to create more child-oriented urban housing environments with safe play space.

■ Years 6-8 and beyond

Most societies regard six to eight as appropriate years to begin formal schooling. But children's natural approach to learning and their developmental processes do not suddenly change. In countries where primary school systems are very formal, there is a particular need to provide opportunities to enrich what can be a stultifying process through recreation and out-of-school experiences.

Lebanon: SCF works with young children in the disrupted conditions created by years of civil war and Israeli attacks. The very formal primary school system makes little contribution to helping these children develop confidence and emotional security. SCF supports a range of out-of-school and holiday activities which help to fulfil this need, and has developed a Child-to-Child health education project – an approach which gives children the experience of active learning that school does not offer.

Laos: SCF works through the Ministry of Education in Laos to support the reform of both pre-school and primary teacher training – to encourage more active learning approaches based on a better understanding of how children learn.

specially vulnerable children

In all its work, SCF aims to reach the most vulnerable and marginalised groups. The biggest single cause of vulnerability is poverty but, since poverty is so widespread, SCF focuses on specific groups of children because of scarce resources and the need to make an effective impact. Among the groups SCF's programmes have worked with are: children of migrant workers; refugees and the displaced; children from remote rural regions and tribal areas who are denied access to basic services; children in institutions; and children in conflict and violent situations.

UK: In London, SCF's Hopscotch Asian Women's Centre supports families, particularly women and children, recently arrived from Bangladesh. Most families experience homelessness and poverty on their arrival. A problem highlighted by the education service is that Bangladeshi children do not do as well in school as they should. SCF, in partnership with education agencies, is developing out-of-school clubs, family literacy programmes and parent participation initiatives, including language skills, to enable parents to speak up for their children at school. As a result parents are better able to support their children's development, and also to influence the way services are provided to support them.

Children who are often excluded

Whichever group SCF works with, it is important that the programme does not collude in denying opportunities to those whom society often excludes. It may be necessary to include specific training to raise awareness of the impact of discrimination, and to develop ways of ensuring equality of opportunity for children.

India: In many regions there are communities described as 'tribal'. They are ethnically and culturally different from the majority community, and usually have very limited access to education, jobs, etc. SCF in India supports a number of NGOs which work with tribal communities. Pre-schools often form a key part of their activities, with dramatic effects on later school attendance and success.

Pre-schools are often seen as a preparation for school, therefore an early childhood programme which ensures that girls are fully included can be a powerful agent in giving girls a better chance of learning opportunities later on. Parents' attitudes are the key to change here. If it is a priority of the project to include girls in pre-schools, it will be essential to involve the parents at all stages.

Access and abilities

One group of children who are very often excluded are those with obvious differences, be they physical, sensory, learning or behavioural. It is a challenge for all early childhood programmes to make positive efforts to ensure that such children have equal access.

It is important to distinguish between the access needs of children with physical disabilities, and the educational needs of children who have some sort of learning difficulty. Children with mobility difficulties may not be able to travel to the centre where the early childhood programme is offered, or once there may not be able to use all the facilities. Special help may be needed to overcome these practical problems. However, access is much more a question of attitude. Many children are excluded because of fear of difference. The first task is to help change the attitudes that exclude.

Adults may need space to discuss honestly what they feel and fear about including such children. This is the adults' problem, not the child's. If we feel 'disgust' at a child who looks very different, it is not the child who is disgusting, but our own attitudes that need to be challenged.

> *UK:* In Birmingham, SCF set up Play Choice, a partnership project with the local authority to raise awareness of disability issues in health, education and social services. Working with disabled peoples' organisations, the project starts by helping childcare workers to identify and question their own attitudes to disability. Building on their existing professional knowledge and experience of child development, the project then supports workers in making changes to their care programme, to their curriculum content and to the environment, so that all children can be included on an equal basis in the services they provide.

Special needs and special skills

Teachers and education authorities often think that special skills are needed to teach disabled children. However, in general 'special teachers' simply use a lot of observation, creative thinking and experimentation. These skilled techniques are usually the kind that would benefit all children: individual attention, lots of encouragement, awareness of what the child can already do and what is difficult for him or her, and practical strategies about how to make things easier. Children themselves can come up with inventive ways of adapting activities so that those who cannot walk, see, or hear may take part.

> *China:* SCF has worked with the Anhui Provincial Education Commission to integrate disabled children into mainstream kindergartens and primary schools. Emphasis is placed on building strong partnerships with families so that school and family work together. The project has focused on changing current teaching practices to improve the early education of *all* children within the kindergartens. The new teaching methods transform the traditional teacher-dominated classroom to one in which children work in small groups, and where play activities and high levels of interaction are encouraged.

Self-image and acceptance

Like every other child, a disabled child needs to be able to accept who he or she is, and feel accepted and valued Disabled children and their parents will often benefit from unsegregated contact with children similar to themselves, and other disabled adults, to promote positive role models. If any resources – toys, pictures, story books, etc. – are available they should also reflect positive images. And just as with other children, the more the experiences of home and pre-school are linked, the greater will be the positive impact. Parents of a disabled child may be subject to fears of society's judgement on them for producing such a child. They may need help and encouragement to understand that the child can learn, and in which ways they can help him or her.

3. CREATING AN ACTIVE LEARNING ENVIRONMENT

It should be clear from all that has been said that creating a positive environment in which children can develop is a complex task which needs to involve, and draw on the understanding of, all the adults who are close to those children. But there is also a need for specific training for childcare workers. It takes considerable skill to set up learning situations in which each child can progress at his or her own pace, and it is unrealistic to expect childcare staff to be able to do this without training.

What type of training?

Some approaches to training are considerably more effective than others. It is easy to be misled by an enthusiastic response. People may enjoy a training course yet still continue to work in the same way as before. They may consider that what they have learned cannot be easily applied in their situation. They may perhaps have been exposed to the new approach too rapidly, and not have been able to make it their own.

New approaches to learning and child development are not issues that can easily be imparted on a short training course. Carers, teachers and other members of a community need repeated opportunities to develop and test out new approaches for helping children learn, and to reflect on their practice. The essential component of such training should be practical: observing what children already know, are aware of or can do, and what they show interest in trying to do next.

West Bank/Gaza: The impacts of war, political change and military occupation have all contributed to disrupting family life. In this situation, SCF supports training workshops for women in local community groups who care for young children. They have found that many of the women themselves need to experience the creative possibilities of play before they can be trained to improvise and create equipment and to understand how young children

learn. The training programmes give them a chance to analyse feelings, and to discover and experiment, with practical activities to enable them to appreciate the difference between a child's and an adult's point of view.

What type of equipment?

Western-designed and bought items of pre-school equipment can develop their own magic significance for pre-school workers in poor communities, signifying that they are giving children the 'best' opportunity. It is important that the training process does not leave the impression that these items are essential for learning.

■ Learning materials are all around you

Children are stimulated by any object that is new or different. They do not need bought toys. There is no point spending scarce resources buying plastic blocks to teach children to count and to sort sizes and shapes, when the environment around them is full of sticks, stones and seeds which fulfil the same purpose. Furthermore, objects that are familiar to the child say something important when they are used as learning games – they convey the vital message that learning is not a privilege of the rich but a capacity anyone can exercise, anywhere.

Mongolia: In traditional nomadic communities, adults and children play games with collections of small sheep bones as dice, counters, etc. Pre-school teachers have adapted these resources to create many different learning and counting activities for children.

Children need a variety of images to nourish their imaginations and to build their confidence. In societies where children from certain ethnic groups are disadvantaged, it becomes particularly important that they see their community's lifestyle depicted as normal and valued in pictures and stories.

■ Play materials are there to be used – by children

Pre-school workers who receive their first training in active learning approaches may become adept at making things out of paper, card or local materials, but these sometimes end up in a cupboard out of the children's reach – in case they damage them. If this happens, the essential point has been missed. Toys have little value as objects. It is only when children use them that toys can stimulate learning. Pictures or charts on the walls need to be at a height where *children* can see them.

If given the freedom and encouragement to do so, children will invent their own toys, and that in itself is a creative learning process. They will get more benefit from collecting freely available raw material (leaves, mud) and experimenting with making things from them, than from a few objects carefully made by their teacher.

■ Equipment that can be acquired cheaply

Pre-school workers in many different countries have found imaginative ways to provide free or low-cost equipment. All cities produce quantities of industrial packaging or waste products, many of which can be recycled, if safe for children, as materials for children's craft and activities. Paper from offices can be used for writing. In Zimbabwe, for example, farm owners have been persuaded to supply gum tree poles and old tyres (both of which they have in abundance). An SCF project has set up workshops to train villagers in turning these into outdoor play equipment for climbing and swinging.

■ Activities that need no equipment

Some of the most fruitful activities for children require no equipment at all: songs, dances, storytelling or the games children play with each other, with words and with their imaginations. Children also learn by taking responsibility for themselves and for others. A well-designed pre-school will ensure that children begin learning the practical skills they will need for life in their own community.

4. WHAT'S THE IMPACT?

Given the long-term nature of child development, what kind of impact can one expect to see from early childhood programmes? This is a complex question which is perhaps best approached by looking at examples of programmes worldwide, in a variety of challenging contexts, and seeing what effects they have been designed to bring about.

Minimising the damaging effects of poverty

The experience of SCF internationally offers many examples of early childhood programmes being used as a vehicle for tackling the worst constraints of poverty:

India: There are 56 million Indian children under six years of age whose mothers have to work in order to survive. Many children go to workplaces with their mothers – construction sites, quarries, mines. An SCF-supported NGO, Mobile Crèches for Working Mothers, runs crèches on construction sites to provide children with a safe and stimulating environment, and has used this base of practical involvement to negotiate with construction companies to provide basic facilities and more secure working conditions.

UK: The Rosemount Project in Glasgow is a community-based centre which combines childcare and training opportunities to promote SCF's anti-poverty work in an economically depressed area. A variety of courses are offered to women who are lone parents, long-term unemployed or from low-waged families. Trainees are awarded with nationally recognised qualifications to help them get jobs or go on to further education. Each course guarantees access to quality childcare, which gives the children from disadvantaged groups opportunities they would not otherwise have.

Mongolia: Mongolia's economy is under severe stress as it undergoes the transition from a centrally planned economy to a market economy, and the removal of trade subsidies. Childcare is a major issue, as many households are headed by women who have to go out to work, and who cannot afford fees for pre-school places. SCF has identified work with young children as one effective way of contributing to a wider poverty-alleviation programme. By supporting newly emerging local NGOs it has raised public awareness about the needs of children, and has worked with the Ministry of Education to develop a Pre-school Strengthening Programme.

Advocacy for children's needs and rights

SCF's work in several countries has shown how being involved in providing basic childcare can lead to effective advocacy work, which can gradually win some significant improvements for children in disadvantaged communities:

Zimbabwe: Children of farm workers on large commercial farms, where patterns of life have changed little since pre-independence days, are denied access to education because the government does not build schools on privately owned land. SCF's Farm Workers Programme has persuaded farm owners to provide facilities for basic childcare, which has then led to a demand for primary schools to be built on the farms. Programme staff have successfully negotiated between workers, farm owners and government, and continue to play a crucial role advocating the rights of farm children to education and basic health facilities.

Philippines: SCF in the Philippines has experimented with a range of advocacy activities to highlight issues of child rights. One of SCF's roles is to work through government structures to press for rights which exist on paper to be put into practice, such as daycare provision. Another is to support local NGOs which have well-developed early childhood approaches, so that their experience is made available to government outreach workers, to encourage awareness of children's needs and rights.

UK: In Holloway Women's Prison, SCF worked in partnership with the Prison Service to develop a children's full-day visit scheme. This alerted the public to the inadequate visiting arrangements for children, and highlighted the child's right to maintain contact with their imprisoned parent. The Prison Service is now changing its policy to encourage the development of further schemes. A prisoners' children's network is also being developed to offer support, advice and information for children by children.

Children's needs in times of crisis

SCF has a history of responding to emergencies, and then being drawn into longer-term work in the post-emergency phase. In these situations, perhaps more than any other, people working in SCF or similar agencies query whether it is possible to consider the longer-term developmental needs of young children, given that their very survival is in question, and the communities they belong to are under such pressure. SCF's experience indicates that there is a lot that can be done to minimise damage to children at such times.

Let us look at a few examples of work in which SCF has been involved:

■ Emergency feeding, health care

In wars or famine the immediate priority is to ensure that children survive. SCF's first response has usually been to provide emergency feeding and basic health care in refugee camps. During the 1980s and early 1990s there have been major programmes of this kind in Somalia, Ethiopia and Sudan. Currently SCF is responding to the rapidly changing, unsettled conditions in Sri Lanka, Liberia, Rwanda, Angola, among Bhutanese refugees in Nepal, and Burmese refugees in Bangladesh.

■ Family tracing and reunification

After physical survival, the child's most important need is for security and a caring environment. SCF has played an important part in setting up family-tracing programmes in several African countries (Uganda, Angola, Mozambique, Rwanda) and in Bosnia, to reunite children who have been separated from their parents. Where families cannot be traced, children may be placed in substitute families. SCF's experience of this work has enabled it to take a leading role in getting international agencies together to develop guidelines on good practice.

Although these activities may need to be set up rapidly, in the midst of emergency conditions, they can have long-term effects on the children concerned. Nothing is more damaging to a young child than the loss of the permanent loving relationship which, ideally, parents or primary carers provide. If parents or carers have been lost or killed, the child is deprived of the framework of emotional security which is fundamental for healthy development. Helping children to be re-established with adults who can care for them is the single most important support that can be given to minimise the damage done to them in conflict situations.

Rebuilding during and after conflict

Another set of programmes focuses not so much on the individual child, but on supporting the reconstruction of social or economic structures which will enable communities to reassemble, allowing children's lives to regain some semblance of normality.

South Sudan: Civil war has disrupted normal life in south Sudan for much of the past 25 years. SCF is one of the few large NGOs working in the remotest areas, and has supplied seeds and tools to enable farmers to start supporting themselves again. Through this work SCF learned that communities themselves were starting up schools – often under trees and with barely educated teachers. These efforts are now being supported by SCF's work with south Sudanese exiles and other NGOs to supply books and basic teacher training whenever the ongoing conditions of war make it possible to do so. The very existence of schools has a morale-boosting effect, providing some form of social structure – both for the children, and for their communities.

SCF has supported education programmes with young children in a number of other emergency and post-emergency situations: in refugees camps in Hong Kong, supporting pre-schools among Vietnamese refugees; and in Tanzania, with women and children in the camps for Rwandan refugees. In the UK, SCF provided a reception project for unaccompanied refugee children

from Vietnam, followed by work towards family reunification, care and resettlement; and a project among Somali refugees, piloting a combination of quality childcare with literacy opportunities for isolated parents of under-fives. In Lebanon, and in the West Bank and Gaza, SCF has pioneered a variety of approaches to work with young Palestinian children living in very insecure conditions.

A different set of problems arises when emergencies are over, and the media attention (and international funding) has moved elsewhere. SCF has tried to find ways to ensure that children's developmental needs will not be neglected amid all the other pressing concerns facing the new government.

Uganda: A programme of family tracing during the confused post-civil war period led to concern about conditions in children's homes, and subsequently to a long-standing relationship with the Ministry for Social Welfare. This has brought about significant reforms on childcare issues:
- legislation, including a new Children's Bill;
- an ombudsperson for children, from village to district level;
- the closure of many institutions which were disadvantaging children;
- a search for new ways to support children's needs when the impact of Aids makes it harder for extended families to absorb and care for orphaned children.

South Africa: Early childhood work has been a focus of activity for many social activists who were working towards a new political system in South Africa. Since the achievement of political change, activity on early childhood issues has grown rapidly, for people see it as a critical strategy in trying to bring about social and economic change. In several of the projects SCF has supported, developing good pre-schools is seen as one way in which parents and others can act against the 'culture of violence' that exists in marginalised settlements around the cities, or in rural areas dominated by political violence, such as Natal.

In all of these programmes, training has been a major component – for untrained teachers, for those responsible for childcare, for government officials, NGO staff, and others in the community. Perhaps the greatest challenge for all these adults is how to help children cope with distress and come to terms with the disasters they have been part of.

Mozambique: SCF supported work with teachers in an area of Mozambique where many children had been displaced and been affected emotionally by the long-drawn-out civil war. A body of experience has grown out of this work and has since been used in other communities affected by violence – areas such as the Middle East, Eastern Europe and Latin America. Through these training programmes, staff in SCF and partner agencies have become more sensitive to what children are experiencing and to the approaches that could help them come to terms with past difficulties.

Children and the whole community

There are many well-documented cases of early childhood programmes having an impact on wider concerns in the community. SCF's work in India and in the UK provides good examples of situations in which support to local early childhood activities has formed the basis for other development work.

India: SCF supports local NGOs working in remote rural areas, where there are few government services and conditions of life are harsh. Programmes in which the first aim is often to ensure that children will be physically safe and adequately cared for raise issues of community health: access to water, sanitation and general hygiene. Childcare programmes often become vehicles for activities to extend primary health care, from which not only the children but the whole community benefits.

UK: One of the early examples of an SCF initiative having a marked community development impact is the playgroup movement, in which an approach initiated by SCF was taken up as a national example.

In the current demoralising conditions of life in many of Britain's large cities, participating in SCF-supported childcare projects has inspired local people to become active on a range of other community issues.

Education and development – the link

Development work that is genuinely responsive to people's needs will often lead to a focus on children, even where this was not originally intended. In Malawi and Sudan, SCF-supported community development programmes have moved into working with pre-schools because communities said that was one of their priority needs. The pre-schools free the mothers to work in income-generating activities, such as growing vegetables. Pre-schools also allow other siblings (usually girls) who were previously required for childminding to attend school themselves.

People everywhere feel that education has a key role in development. Policy-makers stress its importance in economic development, and in the most disadvantaged communities individuals hope that if *their* children become educated they can escape the trap of poverty by getting a good job. Whether this is likely to happen or not, people cling to the hope. When they realise that the process of learning starts very young, adults begin to press for children to start formal learning at an early age.

However, the links are complex. Research does show that if children arrive at school better prepared, they make better use of the opportunity, and are less likely to drop out. But this only happens if early education fosters their natural developmental processes. Over-formal learning at an early age does not help children escape the cycle of disadvantage.

Changing roles for women

Activities that focus on the young child necessarily create or support changes in women's situations. Most obviously, childcare provision creates different possibilities for the women who normally care for young children. But the links work both ways. A recent policy paper based on SCF's experience in the UK has effectively documented the close connections between training opportunities for women and improved life chances for children. The challenge of setting up and developing early childhood provision acts as a powerful catalyst in enabling women to take a more active part in the community. Many women are child-carers, but the skills of childcare, and the potential for using them more widely, often go unrecognised. When care of young children begins to be seen as a responsibility shared by a wider society, women's skills begin to be valued and needed.

Working with women has to be a key feature of any early childhood programme.

> *UK:* On a low-income housing estate, SCF's Patmore Centre provides community-based services which include daycare and crèches for children, a range of basic skills education and vocational training programmes for women, with parent and community development support. This integrated and flexible approach allows parents to learn skills, and builds their self-confidence so that they can get jobs to support their own families and negotiate on behalf of their children. This approach has now been adopted by a number of local authority family centres that cater for families in crisis.

> *West Bank/Gaza:* SCF's work among Palestinians has a strong training focus, considering personal development of women as essential in ensuring that they will be able to manage and sustain their projects through difficult changing circumstances. The context is one in which women do not traditionally take leadership roles, cannot meet with men easily in public, and are expected to take a passive role in the presence of men. A central feature of the work, therefore, has been to find ways of operating sensitively within this context, while ensuring that women's skills are recognised and that they can take advantage of training opportunities.

> Most of the trainers, coordinators and supervisors are

women. There has been careful attention given to improving literacy levels of trainees, and to developing styles of communication which feel natural to women. The participatory style of training has given women the skills to take part in planning, assessment and evaluation, and confidence that their experience is valued.

5. WHO OWNS THE PROJECT?

Avoiding dependence

Whatever the set of activities, the issue of sustainability must be considered right from the start. Securing funds for good services for children is a worldwide problem, and there are no easy answers. Where lack of funding is the main obstacle, more than anything it is money that local people, communities and governments hope to get from SCF. However, SCF is seldom in a position to provide much funding, and obviously has to find ways of using this money which do not create dependence.

Using limited resources to greatest effect

While financial resources are always a key factor, human resources are even more important. A small budget spent on training key adults in approaches that are genuinely useful can bring about far more positive change than spending the same sum on chairs and tables, even if that is what people asked for. There are many children without any adults to care for them, but without new funding SCF cannot provide more childcare workers. However, there are many strategies for using existing facilities and adults' time so that they will be able to support a larger number of children.

Dependence and ownership

As important as questions of funding are issues of control, initiative and understanding, to ensure that any new awareness lasts and is effectively passed on. No early childhood programme can bring lasting benefits unless local communities – and particularly parents and other carers – are involved in the planning and implementation of the work.

> *India:* In an SCF-supported project in South India the local NGO encourages the development of a community-elected village committee, a village fund and voluntary service to ensure community participation. The village designates a piece of land for the *balwadi* (pre-school). The men from the community dig the foundations and fill the basement, and the NGO provides the materials for a concrete structure. The teachers are selected from the community through the village committee and are sent to the local NGO for training.

An early childhood programme has many potential links with other community activities, but the degree to which these other activities are structured into the programme varies considerably. Making such links as explicit as possible will root the work more firmly in the community's life.

> *India:* In the programme described above, mothers are involved in making learning materials for the *balwadis*, and monthly women's meetings of the village discuss issues such as basic health care for the women and for their children. Health workers visit the *balwadis* every week and any health problems are referred to them. The government immunisation programme is carried out by an NGO health worker and *balwadi* worker. Government teachers and academics are invited to contribute to training courses held at the NGO, and so feel an involvement with the work.

> *UK:* A similar approach has been used in the Buckinghamshire Gypsy and Travellers project. As a result of their mobile lifestyle and the discrimination they encounter, Gypsy and Traveller families may have little or no contact with health or education services. SCF has supported mobile play provision to give play opportunities to young children. Through this contact the needs of women have become apparent and a women's health project and literacy programme has developed, drawing in local workers from the health and education agencies. By involving a range of agencies at the planning and assessment stage, services can be adapted to suit the needs of that community.

Government and community

A crucial factor in ensuring continuity is the 'partnership' arrangements that are set up at the programme design stage, and which continue to be created through a flexible, responsive way of working.

One question which sometimes bothers staff responsible for designing programmes is whether it is more appropriate to be working with governments or with communities. Posed in this way, this is not a useful question. Both or neither may be appropriate, depending on the context. Sometimes the question of scale is important. The countries in which SCF has had most impact on government policies for young children have been small ones. Elsewhere, SCF has succeeded in specific districts where it already has a long record of making useful contributions to supporting the national government's capacity in other areas, such as health. In larger countries, governments are more likely to make partnership arrangements with large donors, or bi-laterally with other governments.

Working in the community may seem at first glance to offer less possibility of influencing what happens for children, except at a very local level. But most governments do not assume responsibility for the care and education of children under school age, so the only pre-school provision that exists is often in the hands of voluntary or community groups. Unlike school systems, these groups may be more flexible in adapting to new challenges. Although voluntary groups do not have the kind of power to affect what happens to children that a government department might have (e.g. through deciding on a new curriculum), they can have an impact on each other by the more diffuse process of spreading ideas. In this type of setting, SCF may have more chance of supporting efforts in ways that will bring real benefits to a large number of children.

What is important is that the decision should be based on a thorough understanding of the local situation, and an analysis of the type of activity most likely to have a beneficial impact. Examples from five countries show the range of approaches with which SCF has experimented:

India: Traditionally SCF has supported the work of many local NGOs, each of which has its own style and priorities. Recently, an early childhood specialist was commissioned to review all the early childhood care and education activities SCF supports in India. The findings are now being used to reassess whether some approaches are more appropriate than others, and to consider if there are ways of linking NGO provision with government initiatives.

Philippines: This is a society with thousands of active local NGOs. SCF started work here only a few years ago, and decided it would be inappropriate to initiate yet another set of activities. But it was noticeable that issues affecting children – here as elsewhere in the world – do not receive high priority. So SCF's approach is to find ways of influencing policies of NGOs, and through them government, to 'think children'.

West Bank/Gaza: For many years, while SCF has worked with Palestinian children, there has been no Palestinian government so the question of supporting government activities or policy development did not arise. The SCF programme has worked creatively to link with most of the organisations concerned with young children, including Palestinian community groups, religious and political organisations and the UN agency UNRWA, in refugee camps, constantly negotiating through layers of the Israeli military and civil administration. The programme is run jointly with SCF (US), linked with a Palestinian University Education Faculty, and working closely with the Arab Resource Collective through which there is a fruitful sharing of experience in the whole Arabic-speaking region. In the changed political context of recent years, it is now possible for SCF's experience to feed into the policy work of the Palestinian National Authority.

Laos: SCF was one of the few international agencies to be active in Laos during the 1980s, at a time when Laos had little outside contact. This led to the Ministry of Education asking SCF if it could provide someone to work with trainers in the pre-school teacher training institute, which was felt to be in need of new ideas. Significant changes have come about, both in training styles and in pre-school teaching approaches – all of which have been enthusiastically taken up. As a result the Ministry of Education asked SCF for support with a similar programme at primary school level. One of the issues for pre-school work is now to look with the Ministry beyond government provision (which reaches a limited number of children, and mostly in towns) to possible community-based approaches for children in more remote areas.

UK: Alongside Liverpool City Council, SCF supports a children's centre in inner-city Liverpool where many families live on low incomes. Park Centre is a good example of simultaneous work at both community and local government levels. The centre provides a model for continuity in childcare and out-of-school support for families and children from birth to 16, in parent and toddler groups, nursery provision, after-school clubs, playschemes and youth groups. The services are developed in partnership with an active local management committee and they reflect the variety of cultures of people who have settled in this port city – including Irish, African and Caribbean. Issues arising from poverty and racism are constantly being tackled through the work of the centre and by initiatives taken by the management committee – including the development of a group, Parents Against Racism In Schools. SCF aims to negotiate a handover to local control which will be acceptable to all and ensure the continuation of high-quality services and support to parents and carers as a way out of poverty. The active involvement of SCF staff has had a significant influence on the city's policies affecting young children, giving more of a voice to parents, carers, those who work in childcare and the children themselves.

Each programme has grown out of the specific challenges created by the context – social, economic, political – and by the role that SCF staff have identified, given what other agencies, government and community groups are already doing.

6. DOES THE WEST KNOW BEST?

What is 'Western'?

SCF is often looked on as a 'Western' organisation which – it is sometimes assumed – can therefore bring 'expert' advice. It is important to be clear about what exactly SCF has to offer. The main distinguishing feature of being Western is having access to a higher material standard of living. It is this fact more than any other that makes Western lifestyles and approaches attractive to people worldwide. But this very fact means that the kind of experience offered by an early childhood specialist from the UK may be irrelevant to people struggling with extreme poverty.

What can a UK-based organisation offer?

The amount of publicly funded childcare in the United Kingdom is the lowest in western Europe, and some estimates put it at below 40 per cent for children aged three and above. By contrast, France, Belgium and Italy all have publicly funded childcare for over 85 per cent of children aged three and above.

Ironically, it is the experience of working in a context where there is *less* recognition of the need for state-provided services that may put SCF in a position to facilitate new approaches based on its UK experience. Where good collective childcare is not likely to be available to many children, one strategy is to work with local communities to develop more informal arrangements. For many years SCF has pioneered innovative community-based alternatives, which are less familiar in societies where there has been stronger centralised planning. Support for good childminding arrangements is one example.

It is a common arrangement in the UK that women who go out to work pay a childminder, who looks after a group of children in her own home. Childminding is not well paid. This means it is often the only affordable option for the mother, but it also means that childminders are often women who have had few opportunities for training. In Manchester, London and other cities, SCF has developed training and support projects for childminders to help them provide a positive and stimulating environment for children. These groups can reduce the isolation of those who care for children, give them chances to share experiences and sometimes equipment (e.g. toy libraries) and opportunities to learn more about child development. Childminders can also gain qualifications, based on their experience, which helps to raise their self-confidence and the status of childminding. In this way childminding can be seen as a valuable part of the childcare sector.

Where there is no money, is experience any use?

SCF works in many countries, therefore it can act as an agent for the creative sharing of ideas:

Hungary: Like many former socialist countries, Hungary has historically had well-developed childcare services for young children. However, the demand for more childcare services for children under four, to support women's return to work, is great. In the transition to a market economy, Hungary now faces a worsening economic situation in which it will be difficult to maintain existing services, let alone expand them. SCF was approached by an organisation supporting daycare centres, which wished to learn from experiences in a country where there has been less central planning, but more community initiative. A partnership project has been set up to bring together key groups within Hungary and a local authority in the UK to develop locally determined and supported childcare services.

The challenges facing 'transition' economies are new to everyone. In this case, SCF has had an opportunity to learn about what was a highly developed approach to childcare, with its own strengths and weaknesses, and to be a vehicle for the exchange of experience with other countries facing similar difficulties.

SCF as a national and international NGO

Internationally, SCF supports local NGOs who lobby on behalf of children. In Britain, SCF itself is a local NGO, carrying out a lobbying role on behalf of children. A current example of this lobbying role is SCF's response to the government's proposed 'voucher' scheme. In an attempt to expand the UK's early-years provision, without committing itself to spending much additional money, the UK government will provide pre-school education vouchers for every child aged four. Parents will be able to spend these on a variety of early-years centres in the private, voluntary or public sector. In fact, the voucher will cover only a limited amount of part-time care and many of the most vulnerable children would be unlikely to be able to make use of this – for example, children with disabilities or those in low-income areas where few childcare facilities exist. SCF has publicly stated its concern about the scheme.

Internationally, SCF has worked in more than 50 countries, in both developmental and emergency contexts. This gives SCF staff a range of experience on the basis of which they advocate on children's issues to governments, and to major international agencies. This dual role as a national and international organisation gives a breadth of experience few agencies share.

One thing SCF's experience reveals is that international agencies are often unduly powerful compared to local groups, and unless they work with great sensitivity can do considerable harm. Early childhood work is – like any other aspect of 'development' – subject to fashions, driven by donors, and in danger of imposing 'solutions' from a position of unadmitted cultural dominance. SCF consciously strives to avoid these dangers, by employing local staff and drawing on their knowledge of local conditions and sensitivity to local issues. It is from extensive international experience that SCF knows there can be no global answers.

CONCLUSION

There is no conclusion, for this is a beginning. We have started a process of sharing what we have learnt from our experience of early childhood work. Please let us know about yours.

JRTHER READING

e resources listed follow the themes of this booklet. We are
:teful to the Consultative Group on Early Childhood Care and
velopment for help in preparing it.

ny of the items are available for reference in SCF's Equality
irning Centre and in the education adviser's office, London.

rt I: THE NEED FOR EARLY CHILDHOOD
EVELOPMENT PROGRAMMES

Principles of Early Childhood Development

rnard van Leer Foundation (1994) *Why Children Matter:
esting in early childhood care and development*. Bernard van
:r Foundation, Netherlands.

fence for Children International and the United Nations
ildren's Fund (1989) *The United Nations Convention on the
_hts of the Child*, Geneva.

IICEF (1993) *Early Childhood Development: The Challenge and
portunity*. UNICEF, New York.

tachi, A, (1989) *Stolen Childhood: the rights of the child*. Polity
:ss in association with North-South Productions and Channel
ir, Cambridge.

Issues of Poverty and Crisis

etley, A (1990) *The Power to Change*.

hen, B. & Frazer, N. (1991) *Childcare in a Modern Welfare
tem*. Institute of Public Policy Research, London.

otberg, E. (1995) *A Guide to promoting resilience in children:
engthening the human spirit*. Early Childhood Development:
ctice and Reflections Number 8. Bernard van Leer Foundation,
therlands.

iders, C. (1989) *Trends in Early Childhood Development
_grammes: A UNICEF Perspective* and *Early Childhood Education:
_nds and Issues in US Policy*. Workshop on Early Childhood
velopment, State Education Commission of China and UNICEF,
jing, Hangzhou, China.

iders, C. (1991) *Facts for enhancing the Development of Young
ildren: A guide for Caregivers*. UNICEF, Beijing.

vs, S. (1995) *Lasting benefits for children: education and
ining for women*. SCF, London.

ers, R. & Hertenberg, R. (1987) *The Eleven who survive: Toward
e-examination of early childhood development program options
d costs*. Discussion paper, Education and Training Series. World
nk, Report No. EDT69, Washington DC.

ers, R.(1988) *Effects of early childhood intervention on primary
ool performance in the developing countries: An update*. Paper
sented at a seminar on the importance of Nutrition and Early

Stimulation for the Education of Children in the Third World.
Stockholm, 6-9 April.

Myers, R. (1990) *Programming for Early Childhood Development
and Health: The Value of Combining Nutritional and Psycho-
Social Interventions and Some Ways to do it*. Digest No.30
prepared for the UNESCO-UNICEF Cooperative Programme, Paris.

Myers, R. (1991) *The generalization of Early Childhood Education*.
Paper for the Sixth Monograph Week organised by Fundación
Santillana, Madrid, Spain.

Padayachie, R. et al (1994) *Report of the South African Study of
Early Childhood Development: Recommendations for Action in
Support of Young Children*. Centre for Education Policy
Development, Johannesburg and the World Bank, Washington,
DC.

Richman, N. (1995) *Principles of help for Children involved in
organised violence*. Save the Children Working Paper No.14, London.

Schweinhart, L.J. & Weikart, D.P. (1993) *A Summary of Significant
benefits: the High/Scope Perry Preschool Study through age 27*.
High Scope, UK

World Conference in Education for All (1990) *Meeting Learning
Needs in the Period from Birth to the age of School Entrance*. Paper
presented for a roundtable on "Community-level innovations in
Early Childhood Care and Primary Education", World Conference
on Education for All, Jomtien, Thailand, March 1990.

Part II: CHILDREN'S LEARNING AND HOW TO SUPPORT IT

1. Understanding How Children Learn

Bee, H. (1992) *The Developing Child*. Harper Collins, London.

Bonati, G.(1994) *Child to Child: A resource book*. Save the Children
Conference Report, London.

Bruner, J. & Haste, H. (eds) (1987) *Making Sense: The Child's
Construction of the World*. Methuen, London.

Donaldson, M. (1987) *Children's Minds*. Fontana, London.

Dunn, J. (1988) *The Beginning of Social Understanding*. Blackwell,
Oxford.

Goldschmied, E. & Jackson, S. (1992) *People under 3*. Routledge,
London.

Holt, J. (1991) *Learning all the time: How small children begin to
read, write, count and investigate the world*. Education Now
Publishing Co-operative, Derbyshire.

Light, P. & Shelden, S. & Woodhead, M. (eds) (1991) *Learning to
Think: Child Development in a social context*. Open University,
Routledge, London.

Roberts, R. (1995) *Self Esteem and Successful Early Learning*.
Hodder and Stoughton, London.

Smith, P.K. & Cowie, H. (1991) *Understanding Children's Development*. Blackwell, Oxford.

Sylva, K. & Lunt, I. (1994) *Child Development: A First Course*. Blackwell, Oxford.

2. Early Learning and Traditional Education

Athey, C. (1990) *Extending thought in Young Children: A Parent Teacher Partnership*. Paul Chapman, London.

Baker, C. (1993) *Foundations of Bilingual Education and Bilingualism*. Multilingual Matters Ltd, Warwick.

Bertram, A. & Pascal, C. (forthcoming) *Developing a Quality Curriculum for Young Children*. Paul Chapman, London.

Bredekamp, S. (1992) *Developmentally Appropriate Practice in Early Childhood Programs Serving Children from birth through to age 8*. National Association for the Education of Young Children (NAEYC), Washington, DC.

Bruce, T. (1987) *Early Childhood Education*. Hodder & Stoughton, London.

Bruce, T. (1991) *Time to Play in Early Childhood Education*. Hodder & Stoughton, Sevenoaks.

Cazden, C. et al (1990) *Language Planning in Preschool Education*. Harvard University, School of Education with the International Development Research Centre, New York.

Central Advisory Board of Education Committee on Early Childhood Education (1989) *Linkage between early childhood care and education and primary education*. New Delhi, India.

Curtis, A. (1986) *A Curriculum for the Pre-school Child: Learning to Learn*. NFER- NELSON, Windsor.

Drummond, M.J., Lally, M. & Pugh, G. (eds) (1989) *Working with Children: Developing a Curriculum for the Early Years*. National Children's Bureau, London.

Drummond, M.J. & Rouse, D. (eds) (1992) *Making Assessment Work: Values and principles in assessing young children's learning*. National Children's Bureau, London.

Moyles, J. (1994) *The Excellence of Play*. Open University Press, Buckingham.

Nutbrown, C. (1994) *Threads of Thinking: Young Children and the role of early education*. Paul Chapman, London.

Pugh, G. (ed) (1992) *Contemporary issues in the early years: working collaboratively with Children*. National Children's Bureau, London.

Pre-School Playgroups Association (1989) *What Children Learn in Playgroup*. Pre-School Learning Alliance (formerly Pre-School Playgroups Association), London.

3. Questions of Culture

Derman-Sparks, D. (1989) *Anti Bias Curriculum*. NAEYC, Washington, DC.

Pre-School Learning Alliance (1991) *Equal Chances: Eliminating discrimination and ensuring equality in playgroups*. Pre-School Learning Alliance (formerly Pre-School Playgroups Association), London.

Lamb, M. & Sternberg, K. & Mwang, C.P. & Brobora, A. (eds) (1992) *Child Care in Context*. Erlbaum Association, New Jersey.

Neugebauer, B. (ed) (1992) *Alike & Different: exploring our humanity with young children*. NAEYC. Washington, DC.

Save the Children (1993) *Educating the Whole Child: A holistic approach to education in the early years*. Save the Children UK/ European Programme, London.

Siraj-Blatchford, I (1994) *The Early Years. Laying the Foundations for Racial Equality*. Trentham, Staffordshire.

Tobin, J., Wu, D. & Davidson, D. (1989) *Preschool in 3 cultures: Japan, China and the United States*. Yale University Press, Connecticut.

Woodhead, M. *Psychology and the cultural construction of 'Children's needs'* in Woodhead, M. & Light, P. & Carr, R. (eds) (1991) *Growing up in a changing society*. Open University Press with Routledge, Milton Keynes.

4. Abilities and Disabilities

Froschl, Merle et al (1984) *Including all of Us: an early Childhood curriculum about disability*. Ed. Equality concepts U.S.

Mitchell, D. & Brown, R. (eds) (1991) *Early Intervention: Studies for Young Children with Special Needs*. Chapman & Hall, London.

Reiser, R. & Mason, M. (1990) *Disability Equality in the Classroom A human rights issue*. Integration Alliance, London.

Reiser R. (ed) (1995) *Invisible Children: Report of the joint conference on Children, Images and Disability*. Save the Children and the Integration Alliance, London.

Save the Children (1994) *Disability and Development: Achievement and Challenge: Reflections on SCF's Overseas Disability Work*. Save the Children, London.

5. Training Packs & Videos

The Child from Birth through Six. A Training package for Field Workers (forthcoming) Bernard van Leer Foundation, Netherlands.

Early Childhood Development: A Programme Manual and Guide for UNICEF Programme Officers. UNICEF & High/Scope Educational Research Foundation, New York.

Early Child Development and Learning Achievement, 1990. A Statistical Wall Chart on Children. Prepared by the UN Statistical

Office in collaboration with UNICEF, UNESCO and WHO, September 1990, New York.

Equality: A basis for good practice (1993) Save the Children, London. (Training Pack)

The Foundation of Human Learning. A video prepared by Nittaya Kotchabhakdi and Robert Myers for the World Conference on Education for All, Jomtien, Thailand, March 1990.

Infants at Work. Video by Elinor Goldschmeid. National Children's Bureau, London.

Our Present is their future – Quality in early childhood education. Video from the British Association for Early Childhood Education, London.

Observing Children Play. Video & Training manual by Save the Children, Morocco.

The Oxfam Gender Training Manual (1995) Training resource. Oxfam, Oxford.

Part III: DESIGNING PROGRAMMES THAT BRING LASTING BENEFITS

1. Policies and Programmes

Bernard van Leer Foundation (1994) *Building on People's Strengths: Early Childhood in Africa.* Bernard van Leer Foundation, Netherlands.

Cannon, C. (1992) *Changing families changing welfare; Family centres and the welfare state.* Harvester Wheatsheaf, New York/London.

Lanyers C. (forthcoming) *International Handbook of Child Care Policies and Programmes: A Review of Policies in 25 Countries.* Cornell University. Greenwood Press, US.

Lanyers, C. (forthcoming) *Trends in Early Childhood Development Programmes: A Developing Country Perspective Yearbook* in Spodek, B. (ed) *Early Childhood Education, Vol 2: Issues in Early Childhood Educational Curriculum.* Teachers' College Press, New York.

Lanyers, C. (1989) *From Theory into Action: The Need for Early Child Development Programmes.* A paper for the Child-to-Child Conference, Nairobi, Kenya.

Myers, R. (1992) *The Twelve who survive: Strengthening Programmes of Early Childhood Development in the Third World.* Routledge, London.

Myers, R. (1990) *Toward a fair start for Children: Programming for Early Childhood Care and Development in the Developing World.* UNESCO. Available in Portuguese, Spanish, Chinese, French, Arabic and Bhasa, Paris.

Myers R. (1991) *The Development of Young Children: Why we should invest and some suggestions about what can be done.* Discussion Paper for the Agency of International Development, Washington, DC.

Myers, R. (1992) *Towards an Analysis of the Costs and Effectiveness of Community-based early childhood education in Kenya.* A report prepared for the Kenya Institute of Education and the Aga Khan Foundation, Nairobi.

Myers R. (1983) *Analyzing costs of Community-based early Childhood Development Projects*: a paper for "Workshop on Evaluation and Costs of Early Childhood Programmes in Latin America and Caribbean". UNICEF, Chile.

Sylva, K. & Siraj Blatchford, I. (1995 forthcoming) *The Early Learning Experiences of Children 0-6 Years: Strengthening Primary Education Through Bridging the Gap between Home and School.* UNESCO, Paris.

2. Children in Need of Support

Aidoo, H.A. & Sohoni, N.K. (1991). *The girl child: an investment in the future.* UNICEF, New York.

Browne, N. & France, P. (eds) (1986) *Untying the Apron Strings: Anti-sexist provision for the under fives.* Open University Press, Milton Keynes.

Ross, C. & Browne, N. (1993) *Girls as constructors in the Early Years – Providing Equal Opportunities in Maths, Science & Technology.* Open University Press, Milton Keynes.

Save the Children (1994) *An Equal Future: A guide to anti-sexist practice in the early years.* Save the Children UK/European Programme, London.

Save the Children (1994) *A Guide to Good practice on Equal Opportunities in relation to Gender Equality in UK fieldwork.* Save the Children UK/European Programme, London.

Save the Children (1995) *Playing Fair. A parent's guide to tackling discrimination.* SCF and National Early Years Network, London.

UN Centre for Human Rights & UNICEF *Girls & Boys on equal terms. Background note No.6, Convention on the Rights of the Child.*

3. Changing Roles for Women

Anderson, J.(1988) *Child Care and the Advancement of Women.* Paper presented at the Expert Group Meeting on Social Support Measures for the Advancement of Women, Centre for Social Development and Humanitarian Affairs/United Nations Office, Vienna.

Association for Women in Development (1988) *Gender Issues in Development Cooperation*: a summary report of a meeting organised by the Association for Women in Development, Washington, D.C: April 11-12, 1988.

Cleves Moss, J. (1992) *Half a World, Half a Chance: An Introduction to Gender and Development.* Oxfam Publications, Oxford.

El-Bushra, J. & Piza Lopez, E. (1993) *Development in Conflict: The Gender Dimension.* Oxfam Publications, Oxford.

Engle, P. (1986). *The Intersecting needs of working mothers and their young children: 1980– 1985*. Paper presented at the meeting on Women, Work and Child Care in the Third World. International Center for Research on Women/Consultative Group on Early Childhood Care and Development, Washington D.C.

Evans, J.L. (1985a) *The utilisation of early childhood care and education programmes for delivery of Maternal and Child health Primary Health Care components: A framework for decision making*. A Paper commissioned by the World Health Organisation, Geneva.

Evans, J.L. (1985b) *Improving program actions to meet the intersecting needs of women and children in developing countries: A policy and program review*. Paper Prepared for the Consultative Group on Early Childhood Care and Development, New York.

Himes, J. & Landers, C, & Leslie, L. (1992) *Innocenti Global Seminar, Summary Report No.3*. July 1992. UNICEF International Child Development Centre, Florence.

Landers, C. & Leonard A.(1992) *Women's work and Child care: A Review of UNICEF Programmes in Nepal, Ecuador and Ethiopia*. UNICEF staff working paper no. 10, New York.

Leonard, A. (ed) (1989) *Seeds: Supporting Women's Work in the Third World*. The Feminist press, New York.

Leslie, J. & Paolisso, M. (eds) (1990) *Women's work and child welfare in the Third World*. American Association for the Advancement of Science and Westview Press, Washington DC.

MacDonald M. (ed) (1994) *Gender Planning in Development Agencies: Meeting the Challenge*. Oxfam Publications, Oxford.

Save the Children (1994) *Opening Doors for women – report on the Guidance, Access and Training for Women in Europe project*. Save the Children UK/European Programme, London.

Save the Children (1995) *Lasting benefits for children: Education and Training for Women*. Save the Children UK/European Programme, London.

Wallace T. & March C. (1991) *Changing Perceptions: Writings on Gender and Development*. Oxfam Publications, Oxford.

4. Reports on Select SCF Programmes

India: An assessment of the Early Childcare and Education Programmes supported by SCF in India. By Divya Lata. September 1995.

Jamaica: Pathways to Parenting: A Caribbean Approach. Volume 2: A Facilitator's Manuel for Parenting Groups. Parenting Partners. Save the Children, UK/Jamaica. (1990)

Laos: Save the Children's Education work in Lao. P.D.R.: Report of a visit May 1994 by Marion Molteno. (Programme Evaluation Report available from mid 1996).

UK: Working with Parents. Save the Children UK/European Programme, London. (1994)

Report on the SCF Centre-Based Family Support Work Seminar (March 1994).

West Bank & Gaza: Report of a visit to Save the Children Early Childhood Development Project, West Bank and Gaza October 1995, by Marion Molteno.

5. Organisations

The Consultative Group on Early Childhood Care and Development publishes "The Co-ordinators Notebook: An International Resource for Early Childhood Development" – details from Cassie Landers, Consultative Group, UNICEF (H2F), 3 United Nations Plaza, New York, NY 10017, USA. Tel: (212) 326-7137.

Other organisations which produce useful resources

Bernard van Leer Foundation
concentrates on the development of low-cost, community-based initiatives in early childhood care and education. Publishes a newsletter, plus other publications. Details from Bernard van leer Foundation, PO Box 82334, 2508 EH The Hague, Netherlands, Tel: (3170) 351 2040.

British Association of Early Childhood Education (BAECE)
111 City View House, 463 Bethnal Green Road, London E2 9QY.

National Association for the Education of Young Children
1509 16th St. N.W., Washington, DC 20036-1426.
Network of American early childhood educators, publishes the journal *Young Children*.

National Children's Bureau
aims to raise awareness of the needs of young children, and promotes good practice through publications and an extensive information service. Early Childhood Unit, National Children's Bureau, 8 Wakley Street, London EC1V 7QE

Organisation mondiale pour l'éducation préscholaire (OMEP)
DCDPE Institute of Education, University of London, 20 Bedford Way, London WC1A 0HH. Publishes the *International Journal of Early Childhood*.

Oxfam Publications (UK and Ireland)
274 Banbury Road, Oxford OX2 7DX, UK

Pre-School Learning Alliance
(formerly Pre-School Playgroups Association)
69 Kings Cross Road, London WC1X 9LL

UNESCO Press
Commercial Services, 7 Place de Fontenoy, 5-75700, Paris.
Tel: (331) 4568 1000